In the series by M. Sasek

THIS IS PARIS (1959)

THIS IS LONDON (1959)

THIS IS ROME (1960)

THIS IS NEW YORK (1960)

THIS IS EDINBURGH (1961)

THIS IS MUNICH (1961)

THIS IS VENICE (1961)

THIS IS SAN FRANCISCO (1962)

THIS IS ISRAEL (1962)

THIS IS CAPE KENNEDY (1963)

THIS IS IRELAND (1964)

THIS IS HONG KONG (1965)

THIS IS GREECE (1966)

THIS IS TEXAS (1967)

© **MIROSLAV SASEK, 1963**
First published 1963: reprinted 1966
PRINTED IN ITALY BY FRATELLI FABBRI EDITORI

M · Sasek

THIS
IS
CAPE
KENNEDY

Macmillan

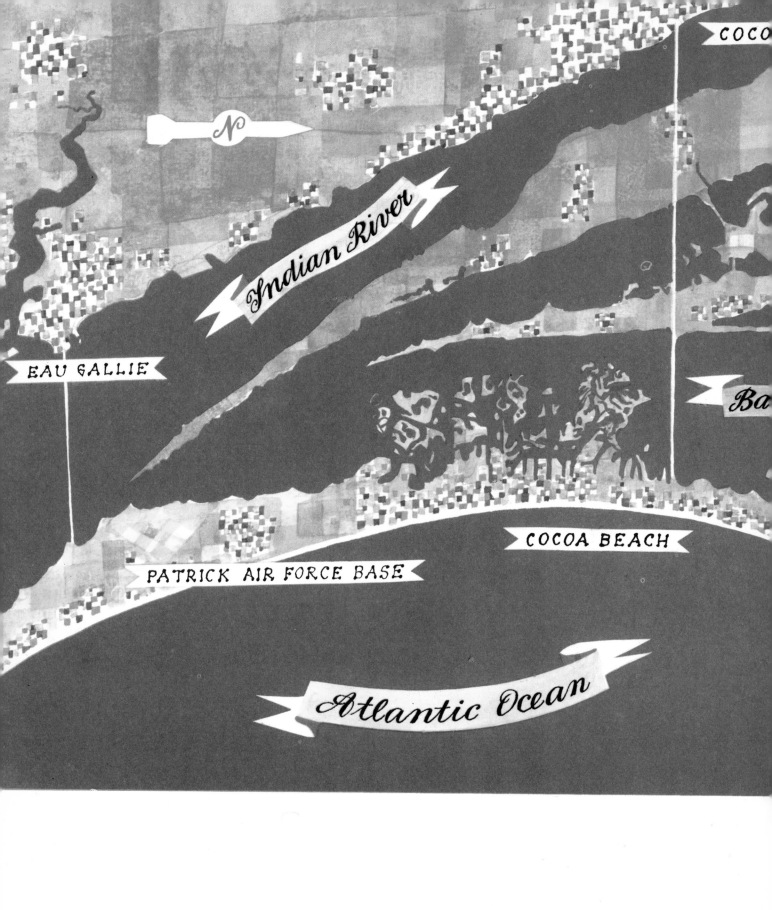

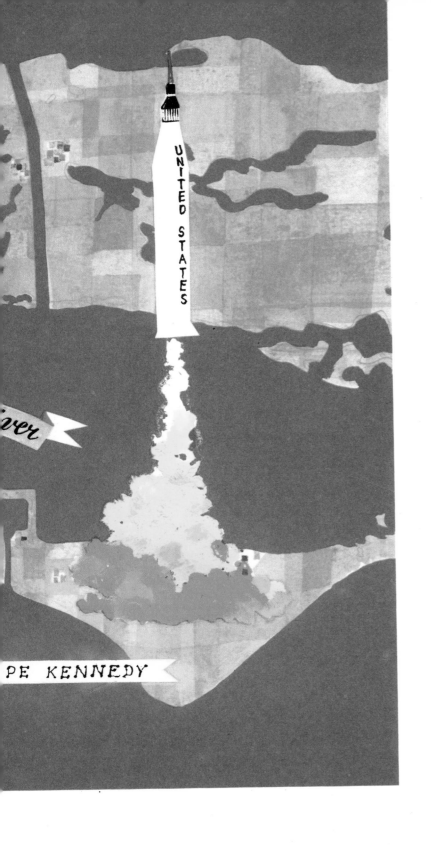

On the east coast of Florida, 190 miles north of Miami, you enter a land of giants, of science-fiction-turned-fact, among whose denizens are the Atlas, the Thor, the Saturn, the Polaris, the Redstone, the Titan, the Jupiter. Their language includes mystic incantations such as AFMTC, ICBM, IRBM, NASA. This is the land of satellites, space vehicles and spacemen, "Space Capital of the World," "Gateway to the Moon," "U.S. Spaceport No. One"—Cape Kennedy.

At Cape Kennedy the effective speed limit is 17,400 m.p.h. A few miles away it is somewhat less. Here you are invited to have "Fun in the sun."

But one day in the sun can get you 60 days in the shade.

When this quiet beach is filled with crowds
staring north, one knows that something historic
is happening at Cape Kennedy seven miles away.

But even at ordinary times one feels the nearness of the Cape.

A sticker for your car—

POST CARDS
6 FOR 25¢

a card for your friend—

the photo shop—

a silver souvenir—

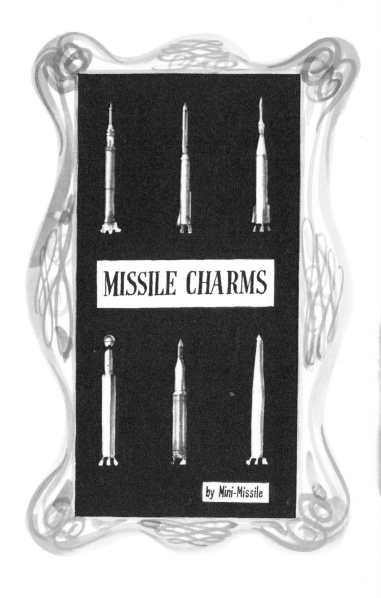

MISSILE CHARMS

by Mini-Missile

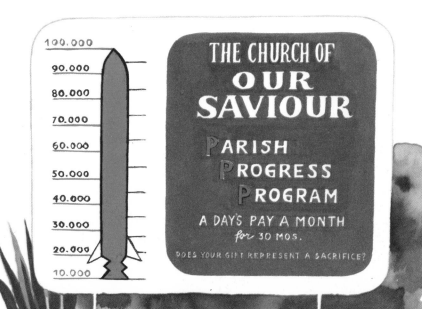

the church.

Here they make doors into portals and spacefolk from small mortals.

Missile REALTY

SU 3-7661

COCOA BEACH
FLA.

WEZY
MOBIL NEWS

Missiles, missiles every-
where—

WHITE CAPS
STEAK
HOUSE

EAT

Missile Taxi

117 COCOA AV

SU 3-7276

and earthly space to let.

"Toast of the Coast in Our Orbit Room."

"Space Flight is Missile Business.
Motel Space is Our Business."

Cape Colony Inn. Some day in this motel there may be a plaque saying: "Here lived the first U.S. astronauts."

In the lobby stands the model of an Atlas. The ancient Atlas carried the world on his shoulders; the modern one carried the first American into orbit.

The only place on the Cape where you can see real missiles at close range is the permanent display in front of the Technical Laboratory at Patrick Air Force Base.

Inside this building are stored thousands of miles of magnetic tape and film, recording all the data from Cape Kennedy flights.

At Patrick Air Force Base is the headquarters of the Air Force Missile Test Center, which operates a dozen stations belonging to the Atlantic Missile Range. This missile test range extends some 10,000 miles over the sea, all the way to the Indian Ocean. Cape Kennedy is Station No. One in both senses of the word.

A leaflet says: "The display lends itself especially well to family photography." This man finds it a bit hard.

US NAVY
POLARIS

LENGTH   28 Feet
DIAMETER 54 Inches
WEIGHT   30.000 Pounds
RANGE   1.200 Nau-mi

US ARMY
PERSHING

HEIGHT: 34 Feet
RANGE: Selective
SPEED: Supersonic
PROPULSION:
  Two-stage solid
      propellant
WARHEAD: Nuclear

To the tourist these may be missiles. In the missileman's slang they are "birds."

Cocoa Beach used to be a small village. In only
10 years it grew at space speed from 273 inhabi-
tants to over 7,000. Cape Kennedy is next
door.

But its door is not too easy to open.

PATRICK AIR FORCE BASE
CAPE KENNEDY MISSILE CENTER
ROAD CLOSED TO PUBLIC
EXCEPT SUNDAYS

Gateway to U.S. Spaceport No. One, officially called Cape Kennedy Missile Test Annex.

Through these portals indeed pass daily only missilemen; the 10,000 scientists, engineers and technicians who work here for the Navy, the Army, the Air Force and NASA (National Aeronautics and Space Administration).

The first missile was launched from here on July 24, 1950.

Since then, over 1,400 space vehicles of all shapes, types and sizes have been fired from the Cape.

This is all there was on the Cape some years ago.

Today nearby there grow forests of antennae which track missiles in flight. Some look like vast celestial combs —

Here is a radar that tracks the missile just for a short while ; 90 seconds after launching, a similar radar in the Bahama Islands takes over.

some like huge spider webs. This antenna is called the "Dish."

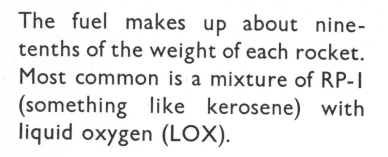

The fuel makes up about nine-tenths of the weight of each rocket. Most common is a mixture of RP-1 (something like kerosene) with liquid oxygen (LOX).

Safety facilities for those handling another of the liquid fuels.

The process of fueling is dangerous and is done only just before launching, as with this Vanguard.

LIQUID OXYGEN

QUID OY GEN

The U.S. Air Force Minuteman was the first American missile propelled by solid fuel.

The Minuteman can be launched from an underground silo —

the U.S. Navy Polaris, from a submerged submarine—

the U.S. Army Pershing, from a mobile erector-launcher.

Titan

height — 100 ft.

weight — 110 tons, of which 100 tons represent fuel

thrust — 300,000 lbs., equivalent to 4,500,000 h.p., or the combined power of 15,300 average-size cars

Rocket-spotters please note: this is a later development of the Titan shown on pages 21 and 22.

Jupiter

On January 31, 1958 this missile launched Explorer I, the first U.S. scientific satellite.

The NASA Saturn —the largest known rocket.

Its first stage, a cluster of eight Jupiter engines, is 21 feet in diameter. Its height is 163 feet, its thrust equals 32,000,000 horsepower. This is the missile that is aiming for the moon.

It is built at Huntsville in Alabama and is transported to the Cape by Saturn barges —

and to the launch site by special trucks.

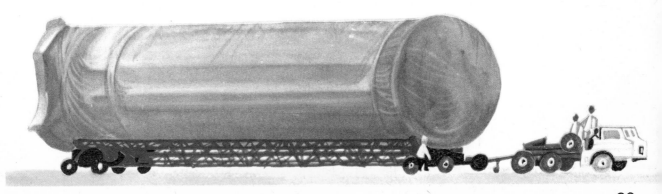

Mercury Redstone
height—83 ft.
weight—33 tons

On January 31, 1961 this missile pro-
pelled a 37-pound astronaut named
Mr. Ham 420 miles down the Atlantic
Missile Range.

On May 5, 1961 another Mercury Redstone propelled a rather
heavier astronaut named Alan Shepard 302 miles down the range,
making him the first American spaceman. His 15-minute flight was
the result of years of preparation and cost $400,000,000.

He is carrying his air conditioner. His space suit is a bit
more expensive than Mr. Ham's. It is made to measure,
consists of 1,300 parts, and weighs 22 lbs. Its cost—$2,000.

The National Aeronautics and Space Administration Project Mercury Astronauts, the first seven U.S. space pioneers.

NASA, a civilian organization, was created in 1958 by an act of Congress. Its overall plans include experiments in physics, chemistry, astronomy, astrophysics, and several space projects of which the first was Project Mercury. The aim of Project Mercury: to put man into orbit and to investigate his ability to perform in space.

All the manned orbital flights have been made by Mercury Atlas. Atlas is built in San Diego, California, and is flown to Cape Kennedy by special aircraft.

Each type of missile has a special launch complex. This one is for the Atlas.

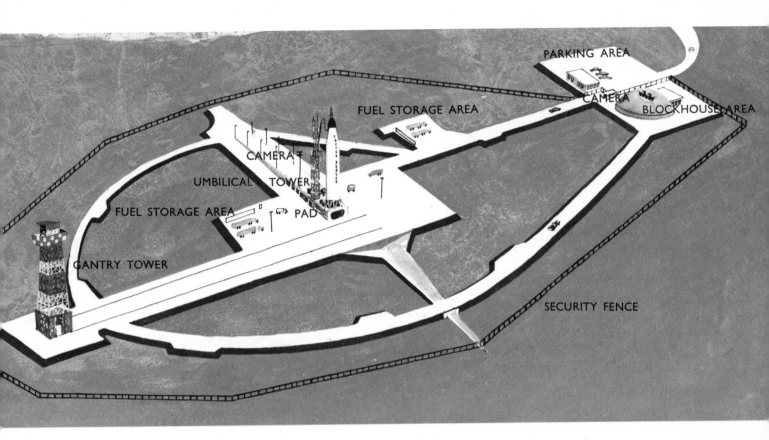

The gantry is a service tower from which the rocket is checked and made ready for lift-off. Before the launching, this vast, many-tiered platform rumbles away on its rails to its parking area.

The umbilical tower keeps the missile "alive" on its pad just prior to flight.

The blockhouse is a reinforced concrete bunker from which the firing of the missile is directed.

Everybody entering the launching area must wear a helmet.

Mercury Atlas with its spacecraft during pre-launch checkouts:
height—93 ft.
weight — 264,000 lbs., including 235,000 lbs. fuel
thrust — 360,000 lbs.
speed — 17,400 m.p.h.

The red device on top of the spacecraft is the escape tower. It is provided with a powerful rocket which, in case something should go wrong before launching, could lift the capsule off the Atlas and parachute the astronaut safely down. After a successful launching, this tower drops off at about 50 miles altitude and burns up.

Now the gantry tower has been moved away and the astronaut is quite alone in his capsule. His last connection with earth before his flight into space is the cord of the umbilical tower and the voice from the control room during the final stages of the countdown.

That voice comes from the blockhouse.

This is how the control room looks during the countdown. There are no windows here at all. Engineers and technicians can watch the rocket only on TV screens or by periscope.

The big bird lifts off.

During the first minute of its flight the Atlas consumes more fuel than a jet airliner during a flight from New York to London.

Now begins the astronaut's lonely journey into space.

"Birdwatchers" at the Cape's press site. Thousands of others, usually less well equipped, crowd Cocoa Beach, and millions more throughout the country do their bird-watching by television.

The Mercury spacecraft looks like a television tube, and is made like a thermos bottle so as to keep cool inside. It is 10 feet high, 6 feet in diameter, and weighs one ton.

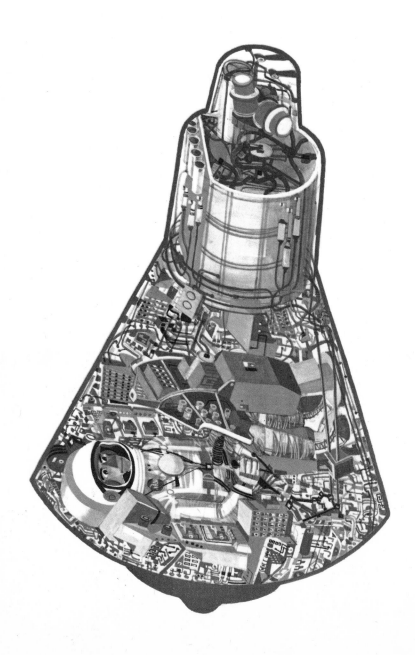

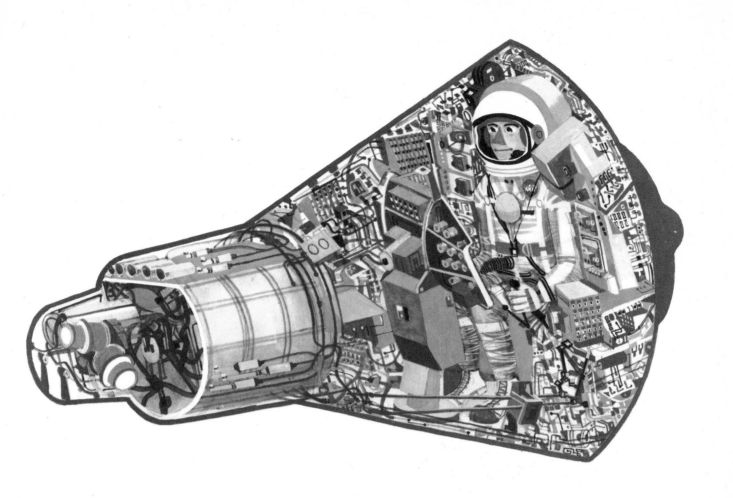

The capsule separates from the Atlas at an altitude of 100 miles and is turned by small rockets to fly with the broad heat-shield forward. At that moment its speed is 17,400 m.p.h. To complete one orbit of the earth takes 90 minutes. Each orbit carries the astronaut through the full cycle of day and night.

Immediately after the launching of the Atlas, Mercury Control Center, a couple of miles away, takes over from the blockhouse and becomes the brain of the entire mission. With the help of the tracking stations all over the world, these men have complete control over every detail of the flight: the capsule and the condition of the astronaut up to his re-entry into the atmosphere, and the recovery of the man and his spacecraft.

All tracking stations and key information from them are displayed on this World Map:

CTN	Canton Island	CK	Cape Kennedy	ZZB	Zanzibar
HAW	Kauai, Hawaii	BDA	Bermuda	IOS	Indian Ocean Ship
CAL	Point Arguello, California	ATS	Atlantic Ocean Ship	MUC	Muchea, Australia
GYM	Guaymas, Mexico	CYI	Canary Islands	WOM	Woomera, Australia
TEX	Corpus Christi, Texas	KNO	Kano, Nigeria		

40,000 people worked on Project Mercury. Of these, 15,000 were engaged on the recovery, using 30 ships and hundreds of aircraft.

THE COCOA TRIBUNE

16 Pages Today

VI No. 155 - Ést. 1917. Cocoa, Brevard County, Florida Wednesday, October 3, 1962 Published Daily Monday thru Friday - 5c a copy

Longest U.S. flight
STRONAUT
GOES INTO
4TH ORBIT

Takeoff Beautiful As Atlas Boosts Capsule Skyward

World-Telegram
and he Sun
...today. Fair tonight. Sunny, mild tomorrow.
EDNESDAY, OCTOBER 3, 1962 TEN CENTS

EARLY **WALL ST.** PRICES

Le cosmonaute U.S., tourne autour de la Terre
Il doit être récupéré en mer au terme de six révolutions

IS ORBITING

'I Feel Real Good,'
Astronaut Reports
As He C...

JORNAL DO BR.
Rio de Janeiro — Quinta-feira, 4 de outubro de 1962

ASTRONAUTA DOS EUA VOLTAS À TERRA E DES

وولتر شيرا يعود سالماً من الفضاء
بعد ان قام بالدوران ٦ مرات حول الكرة الارضية

Herald
NEW YO...
European Edit...
PARIS, THURSDAY, OCTOBER 4

Orbits Six Times, ...
U.S. ...

THE NEWS
No. 12,207 ADELAIDE: THURSDAY, OCTOBER 4, 1962 Registered in Australia for transmission by post as a newspaper.

Astronaut jun. Big grin
CAPE CANAVER...
(AAP-Reuter): Ameri...

5 ¾ on

NACION
JEVES 4 DE OCTUBRE DE 1962 24 PÁGINAS San Martín 344/60 - Florida 337/47 - 49-7201 y 40-40...

ciones
Gran hazaña espacial de los Estados Unidos
SEIS VUELTAS A...

Deutsche Zeitung
Ausgabe M • Preis 30 Pf.
E NACHRICHTEN AUS POLITIK · KULTUR · WIRTSCHAFT · SPORT
München, Donnerstag, 4. Oktober 1962 B 7979 A Nummer 238
Erfolgreicher Raumflug der Amerikaner

Sie lesen heute
Generäle jonglieren mit der Macht
Indonesiens Armee will die Parteien aus-
manövrieren / Von Hans Keiser . Seite 3

נחת בשלום
דור הארץ שש פעמים

ie Transvaler

Prys: 3c

Telefoon 44-9182, Posbus 8124, Johannesburg.

e Jaargang. Nr. 4. ★ DONDERDAG 4 OKTOBER 1962

AS NUUSBLAD BY DIE HOOF-POSKANTOOR INGESKRYF

ONS SPORTAFDELING SPESIALISEER in Die Hersnaar en Herstel van Tennis-, Muurbal- en Pluimbalrakette

UNIEWINKELS PRETORIA

200,000 Myl afgelê

MAN LAND VEILIG

So lyk hy

B·Z·

15 Pf A 2032 A

Nr. 232 · 86. Jahr / Berlin, Donnerstag. 4. Okt. 1962

Die größte Zeitung Berlins

Sechsmal die Erde umkreist

Grad

Landu

My sweet little bird

—SAYS SPACEMAN

ידיעות אחרונות

ליל ולנוער

12 אגורות

הרגשתי מצוין", - מספר ג

„הוא נראה בריא כמו דב", — אומר הרופא

„..לא רציתי למות לפני ז

The Advertiser

WITH WHICH IS INCORPORATED "THE REGISTER."

Adelaide, South Australia, Friday, October 5, 1962.

Audited Net Exceed 191 'Daily

OVER SALES WID

ORBITS "A MILK RUN" NOW, SAYS ASTRONAUT

From GARRY BARKER

NEW YORK, October 4.

"This is really a milk run now," crowed America's fifth spaceman as he whirled over the Indian Ocean at 17 500 m.p.h. yesterday, riding upside down, eating his

The Ottawa Citizen

120th Year, Number 997   Ottawa, Canada, Wednesday, October 3, 1962   5 Cents, 68 Pages

DISTRIBUTOR OFFICIAL BOY SCOUTS SUPPLIES ASSOCIATION

Another Space Trip Going Well

York Times.

THURSDAY, OCTOBER 4, 1962.

10 cents beyond 50-mile zone from New York City except on Long Island. Higher in air delivery cities.

RBITS EARTH SIX TIMES, NEAR CARRIER IN PACIFIC LMOST FLAWLESS FLIGHT

A LONGER TRIP DUE

Abendzeitun

24 0111

Jahrgang Nr. 227 * München, Mittwoch, 3. Oktober 1962 * B 1017 A * Preis 20 Pf * 5 1.

Astronaut S In 9 Stunden 6mal

HOME DELIVERY is more convenient. Have The Gazette delivered to your door every morning

Call UNiversity 6-3561 Circulation Department

185th YEAR

The G

48 PAGES   MONTREAL, THURSDAY

'Hallelujah To Latest

Space Exploit Beamed To Europe Via

The Montreal Star

MONTREAL, WEDNESDAY, OCTOBER 3, 1962

Confident Astronaut

Blastoff Into History

EL TIEMPO

BOGOTA, COLOMBIA, JUEVES 4 DE OCTUBRE DE 1962

Apartado Nacional Aéreo

AÑO 51 — No. 17.693   24 Páginas y 8 en Colores — 30¢

EL TIEMPO ESTA AL SERVICIO DE LOS IDEALES DE FE DEMOCRATICA Y SOLIDARIDAD PATRIOTICA QUE EL FRENTE NACIONAL PRECONIZA, Y A CUYO AMPARO LOS PRINCIPIOS CONSAGRADOS EN LA CARTA DE LOS DERECHOS HUMANOS, COMO FUEROS DE LOS PUEBLOS LIBRES, HAN DE SER REALIDAD CONSTANTE PARA TODOS LOS COLOMBIANOS

Vueltas a la Tierra dio Schirra

le Dietas

uelo Perfecto Realizó el Astronauta de E.U.

ancias fisc· ... que atronta do el Congreso.

acepta las objeciones presidenciales. Si el parlamento

ras y trece minutos perimento. — Recu- perfectos condicio-

Miércoles 3 de Octubre de 1962

Nº 19.721 - 14 Págs. - 30 Ctvs.

EL ESPECTADOR

EDICION VESPERTINA

ing St

WEDNESDAY, OCTOB

rbits

Vuelo Orbital Perfecto

Next morning Cape Kennedy (then called Cape Canaveral) became a household name in every language.

The astronaut has fulfilled his mission and put on his civilian clothes again. After the big official receptions in Washington and New York, little Cocoa Beach also welcomes its hero.

And two local specialists in confectionery construction build him a chocolate spacecraft. Many of the same people who worked so hard to preserve the original capsule will happily help to destroy this one.

Then for a while the beach again becomes quiet and sleepy. There is nothing happening.

Or is there? A tiny tourist from Manhattan is about to fly to Moonhattan.

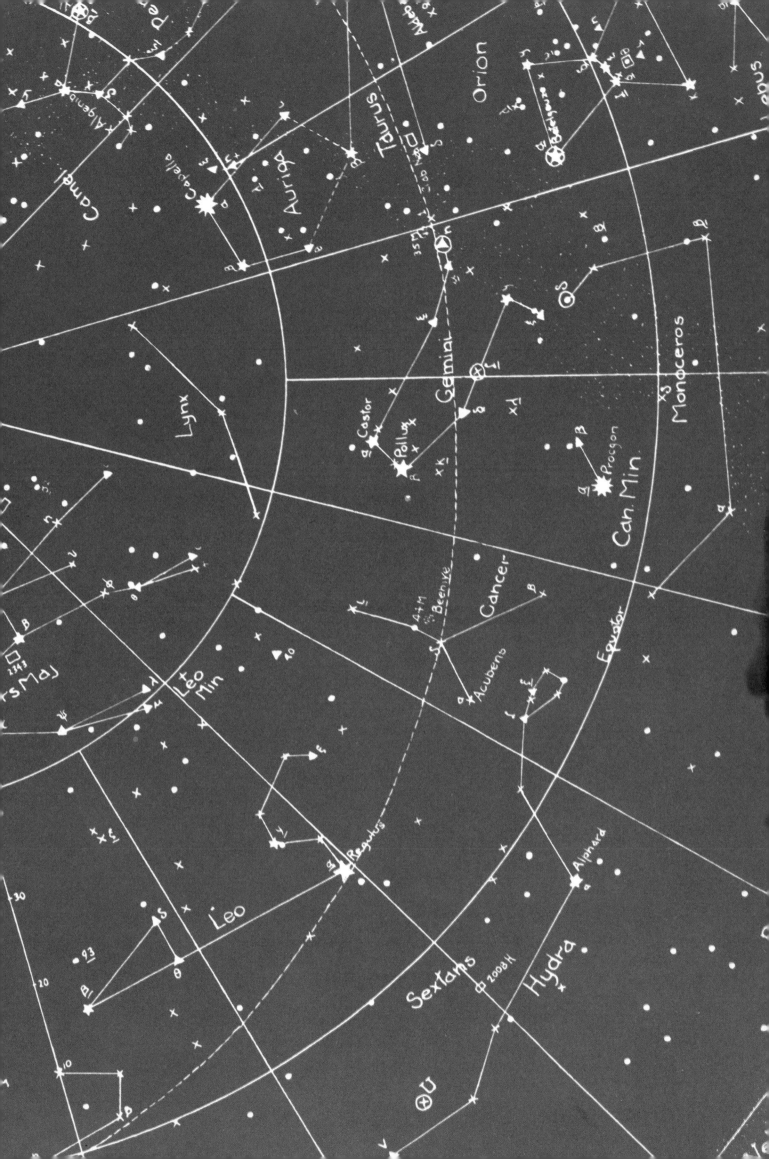